Beautifully Chaotic

Danielle Holian

Written by Danielle Holian
Cover Design by Chika Delaney

ISBN: 9781791639761
Imprint: Independently published

For the arms that hold me;
I love you even though at times
it's hard to love me back.

There is a poem in my bones
A song in my heart
A painting in my blood
And I would be lost without my inner ruins
That make my life art.

Contents

Destruction

Brewing Up a Storm

When life becomes calm
I sit and wait in silence
Surrendering the pain in anticipation
Quietly waiting for the next storm.

Four Walls

Once I close my eyes
The flashbacks come back to haunt me.

I am frightening lying away in the silence
As I watch my room filled with dust.

The memories flash through my mind
To remind me I was once never alone.

And as I close the doors
It's just me and these four walls.

Hide the Truth

Their absence tore me
apart from a young age.

Instead of holding me together
dismissing the rage.

It taught me how to be alone
And never to long another.

And how to survive spending
a lifetime hiding the truth.

Crumble

This dark shade painted over a part of me
Isn't what embedded the anxiety and panic in me.

It's the shame of how someone can crumble me up
like a piece of paper and discard me.

War and Revolution

The war and revolution in me
Taught me from early on
That life is cruel without love
And sometimes pain is created and birth
Instead of life.

Selfish

I come from a place
Where separation is embedded in my blood.

Of people who don't talk
Living on through silence.

It starves my being
And suffocates my expectations.

My screams and time
Go unnoticed and are disapproved of;

I was never enough to satisfy
Their selfish needs.

Absent

A child should never feel
The absence of a parent.

Community

I never had a community around me;
Everyone left after the world crushed at my feet.

No one stayed around to help pick up the pieces;
They were not capable of coping through tragedy.

They acted like my life was a movie;
Only sticking around for the good things.

Instead of loving me through the difficult
circumstances; Not thinking 'one day this could be me'.

No one shows up for me.

Patronising

They talk down to me
Rather than talking to me
In a hardship relationship
Where I am the cause and effect
Of their pain
Oh, so they tell me.

I am ashamed
That the blood in my veins
Connects me to immoral souls
That rumble through the world
Unconscious, yet conscious
Of the hurt, they inflict on me.

Blooming Fear

When he tells me
He yells at me out of love
And his swords of words aren't aimed at me

What else am I to think?
When this endless cycle
All my life only taught me

Men who love you
Abuse their right to
Bloom love instead, put fear in your eyes.

Poison

He tells me I'm wrong
to see the love in the world.

That every person laid
upon me is out to get me.

That who they say
they are is a lie.

Making me think every
person I meet is
poison.

Unresponsive

He stands there in front of me
Screaming and throwing unnecessary words
And it works for a moment before I pull myself back
I see I am not the problem
Or a mirror of his reflection
Or the cause of his pain
When he sees anger, frustration, and hurt
He is too far gone to see the beautiful world around him
But stuck in the past life that he lived through.

He is still there
And I am here in a present
Where the person before me is trying to destroy me
And the actions of his words cut me deep
Like a sharp bladed knife
And I do not reply for the simple fact
I have nothing to say
And nothing I think is worthy
No response would greatly end this tragedy
I am frozen and silenced, again.

Stuck

I could sleep for days on end
But I am awake through it all
Unconscious to the world around me
But stuck in the past that still haunts me.

Shrinking

I curl up;
Knees to chest.

I feel small;
I'm disappearing.

As long as I stay still.

Anxious Disruptions

This reality is suffocating me
I feel like I'm drowning inside
I'm thirsty for a peace of mind
And hungry for a refreshed heart
The stress is slowly dragging me down
Their energy kills my vibe
I'm too young to die
So I stride
Gliding across the floor like a dancer
But I can't take much more
I feel stuck in a moment of uncertainty
Trapped inside this darkness
There is no escape
But plenty of anxious disruptions.

Nothing

I am vulnerable, always seeking validation
To feel like I am more than a lost soul
But I am weak to the liabilities wants and needs
All that is said and done behind their masks
In such a way my heart is betrayed
My mind is fazed in a phase I do not feel enough

Paralyzed in these sad moments
The unfortunate time is what mould me
Into the person I become
Their selfish hands never raised me
Just taught me what I should not be
And I am grateful being an outcast

I struggle to understand addicts love and hate
The rejection, heartbreaks and lost time
And I need to escape this picture perfect presence
I try to please them because without their judgment
I feel nothing
I feel like I am nothing.

Domino Effect

I was taught from a young age
That anger is kindness

So when I fell into the hands
Of someone alike to his character

He saw his reflection in my lover's eyes
But never flinched or seen his actions were wrong.

I learned to trust men just like him
Who hurt me like the way he does.

False Hope

He gave me false hope
That I cling on to.

It hurt more than his temporary existence
Causing permanent damage.

Tiptoe

I lye still next to you
As you finger my spine
Tiptoeing one step at a time;
This is another way for you to walk all over me.

Empty Wishes

I wish he loved me
Rather than loving the body next to him
Once he felt me close
And caressed his on mine
All else was forgotten.

Fight or Flight

My body laid there
Beside him in silence
After screaming no

He said it was okay
That it was expected of me
But I did nothing

I wasn't ready
I did not want to
I tried to fight but froze

The loveless action he portrayed
In front of me was
Rape.

The Little Things

Men have unzipped my body
Removing my clothing and jewellery
Sparing the time to get in between my legs.

But never once do they give me the time of day
To sit down and unravel my mind
Rather than fussing over the little things.

Drowning in Sadness

The silence is crippling
The loneliness is torturous
The white noise tries to drown your voice
But I still hear you.

And if this sadness was water
I'd drowned
Overflowing on the endless road
That led us here.

In the middle of nowhere
And you were the first to run
Leaving me behind
Again.

Unnatural

I never could draw the line
Or let you go.

I never knew how to walk away
Or turn me away from you.

It was unnatural.

Kiss of a Fist

He saw love as an attack
When I held him close
And he fought the truth
Putting me through more trauma
That I may never heal from.

He lost me in the worst of ways
Killing his ability to love
And when I tried harder
I was met with a kiss of a fist
Making me flinch, too.

The Making of Us

I cut pieces of myself away
For each person to fit.

But I disappear
In the making of us.

Unsteady Hands

I tried to pour myself into the hands
Of a man who was not ready for love.

Growing Fear

The boys scattered in the memory of my past
Remain hidden like the naked posters of me
Hung beside their bed
As the last thing, they see before they sleep
And fantasize about what they would do to me.

The world is not a scary place
Only a sharp-edged and delicate surrounding
That allows boys to run wild
And girls to stay inside
Growing fear like hair and body size.

Punchbag

He lost his mind
And tried to find it on my body.

Seconds turned into minutes;
Turned into hours;
Turned into days;
Turned into weeks.

And I never got an apology
For the marks and scars

Dominant

He tells me I'm a breath of fresh air a pretty little thing
That I'm not like most girls
But he alienates me
From my sisters
Under the assumption
I will proudly take his compliment
And praise his wicked ways
But I will not define his actions or faithless words
Of a so called dominant man
Show me what you mean
In a delicate, cherishing, and loving way
Not some quick fire roll of the tongue cheeky response
To get my attention.

Shell

Girls grow into their shells
Ignoring the whispers and whistles across every street
Feeling small and keeping our heads down
These habits and wicked games that some play
Leave scars we never asked for
And from the moment we are born
We are shown our bodies do not belong to us
And sometimes we never heal.

Monster

When I see them walking among us
I see danger
A cemetery with my dead body lying there.

They disguise their urges
Fit into society perfectly
Have their story already written
And an alibi in place as a cover up.

They carved their name deep into my body
Left wounds visible that may never heal
And the invisible ones that I can only see
That will never be forgotten.

I've been defeated and cursed
Left terrified of all mankind
And defined by one in an event that struck many times.

Self Harm

I felt myself self-destructing
When he was here
Close enough to feel my skin on his
As his breath surrendered my body
With every touch, I knew it was wrong
And some sort of misery
That felt like self-harm.

Porcelain

As I try to repair my broken pieces
I realise I am delicate lie porcelain
A shattered piece of art
Motionless as I fade into nothing.

Growing Pains

These bad days, turn into sad days
Going on for weeks on end
And I have grown numb to this pain

These hard hearing thoughts control me
And although I fight through this
It is hard and difficult

I wonder will it ever get easier
Because I am tired, I am exhausted feeling this way
It has taken everything from me.

Powerlessness to Survival

I've encountered heavier things than most
And I've had to learn how to lie
Rather than coming forward each time.

I've had to lie to keep my damaged body moving
Like a puppet on strings
Pretending to be okay when I'm not.

This reluctant feeling of depression drenches the small
forest within me washing away all good inside.

It burns the truth away
As I plant a new path of my life
Creating an alternate universe.

I desperately try to act sane
To feel the flesh on my skin and remember what life was
like before it happened.

But the events erased every inch of me
To a point I no longer recognise myself
And the depression became me

I lost every fragment of my being
And rebuilt my life from the burning ashes
Until my courage and faith grew stronger, again.

Dismissed

They dismiss me every time I try to confide in them
When the suffering overwhelms me
When the hurting painfully opens old wounds
When the layers I covered and healed long ago
Come up to the surface again
And I know they are not transparent or understanding
But sometimes I need empathy and a hand to hold
To reveal my inner true self to someone I love.

A Moment of Near Death

They sugar coat the truth
and it's pointless to sit down
and conversate to explain the pain
and how my heart is heavy
as my mind is full of nightmare-like memories

"Don't make a scene," they tell me
when I came forward, again
feeling like a hostage in a moment
I never wanted to be a part of
and held against my will

"Don't ruin someone's life," they continue
for those short few minutes of him
pleasuring himself on my corpse
could be forgotten in time

But they forget those minutes
have ruined my life
taken my dignity,
the light in my eyes
and the way they look at me
when these handfuls of betrayals happened
All I heard was, "we don't believe you"

I am the disgust in their eyes
the reason their skin crawls
the phone call they expect to pronounce me dead
the taste of bitter that wrinkles their face
The touch so familiar yet foreign

I feel like I'm drowning in an endless ocean from the
moment I surprisingly wake to the moment of near death.

Drowning Out

All the disastrous moments brought to life
During times when I was out of my mind
And high on life
Only see me crash down in full force
And I now see I need to break away from these addictions
That find me surrendering the good parts of life
Diving in fast and drowning out the deafening silence.

Hopeless Romantic

My heart refuses to let go
To let me move on
To explore this newfound world, alone.

I pay attention and take care of myself graciously
Watching the hurt distance itself
From the reality that gradually becomes real, again.

The intense emotions and ache fades
But I remain the same
The hopeless romantic who learns to lives on.

Avoiding Reality

I never believed in love
Back then when a man caught my eye.

I was distracted by the illusion of what it could be
Never what it truly was.

All, in the end, arriving at the same destination
Realising we were just two lonely people;

Avoiding reality.

Red Flags

I question my ways
To love someone emotionally unstable
And worry about the little things
Instead of leaving
And fixing my mind and soul
For my heart breaks endlessly when I care too much
And wonder why people leave
But I give my all, time and time again
And I now see it will never be enough
For someone as incredible as me
To adore someone as weak as them
Previous lovers who wrecked my precious heart
Dragging me down to a level I could not compete with I am
worth more than crumbs they throw
To feed me each time they are bored.

Parallel Universe

In a different creation of my reality
Where I secure a new world around me
I am safe with the power of what happens
To my mind, body, and soul.

As my innocence runs wild
Rushing through my veins
Capturing my sanity
Replacing each emotion with a tender rebirth.

With the pain, suffering, and hurt
Turn into love and find
the light I feel alive
Flourishing my every being and essence.

There's no parallel universe
Where they meet me halfway
I go full force succeeding their wishes
Leaving myself empty.

Purpose

Innocence

Like a child
I find myself wandering into new worlds
With my wide-eyed gaze.

When I turn
My reality is more interesting
With a new perspective and stars in my eyes.

Consuming World

I wait for the day
Where I can feel okay in a mind-set
That does not define my inner ruins
That trap me in this consuming world.

Hope

I fall into the darkness
Wishing every breath didn't come
closing my eyes in fear
And flinch when people touch me.

But something keeps me here
Filling my lungs with air
Through desperate moments
I know I will be okay, again.

Lost Identities

I'm lost in a world of devices
Full of prideful characters with shallow personalities
With lost identities to false personas
With narcissistic actions trapped in a prison of indifference
Feeding on others pain with no helping hands

There are no plans to grow and change
Feeling uncomfortably content staying the same
Remaining powerless in the eyes of an enemy
And all they do is steal our energy
Removing our glows replacing with darkness

In a crowd of blurry faces
The intact sanity unravel the heartstrings
Of a stranger through hate
The scattered meaningless revenge act
Is only a moment to reflect the brokenness inside?

Headphones in blocking out the world
Numbing out, but it's not real
Feel the beautiful trauma of life
As an escape to transport us to a better place
But we are in control to make a powerful change

The silence is loud
The loneliness is consuming
The taste is bitter
The sight is ugly
The smell of the past remains stained

The truth will set you free
But the lies will kill you from within.

All These Years

After all these years
My body still surprises me
With all the neglect, abandonment and self-destruction
My big heart on my little body has gone through trauma
As the invisible scars remain visible on the inside
Through my mind
Damaging my soul
Remaining triggered by body shaming
Hiding away in secret
Yet I stand wholesome wholeheartedly
Brave, scared and empowered
To still fight the urges
Bingeing the pain
Leaving myself on the side-lines
Now I light a match to this wildfire inside me.

Masterpiece

The ink inside your eyes
Paint a world so bright and beautiful
A dreamlike reality
An escape from the real world
And everything in between
A magical moment drew in front of you

Some will try to tear you down
And some will build you back up
Both are a blessing and a curse
From poison to a cure
Don't let the mind of a joker's sour tongue manipulate
Remain tall and unafraid

You will outgrow some things in life
Making room for new beginnings and endings
Know you are worth more than a quick fling
You will cry, turn away and grow distant
But your tears will dry
And the past will fade remaining as a memory

Remain childlike during exciting times
Here in the moment to experience wonderful adventures
Only to flashback to see how far you have come
For you are everything and more when you come undone?
You yourself are art, a masterpiece
An honest version painted upon a canvas

So don't build a life around you
Build a life with you
And never beg for art;
Create it.

Empathy

My greatest weakness is empathy
I'm always there
No matter what state of mind I'm in

I will carry the weight of your problems
Try to fix each issue
While making sure you're okay and safe

But the ones who have burnt me
Scatter the ashes over the mountain of unforgiveness
And come rushing back begging for another chance

And I'm there, I'm always there
Never shielding myself from the careless
Because I know what it's like to be alone

I have to accept this is me
I will always be untangled in this empathy
The need to put others above me

The ones who don't deserve me
are the ones I will never turn my back on
And I think that's what I love most about me.

Untouched by Sorrows

I will never live a life untouched by sorrows
For the ache of blinding heartbreak
Sneaks up on me wherever I go
haunting me in the taunting echo's
Of life before me
Presently
And the unknown future ahead of me.

Voiceless

I may be voiceless
Another lost soul in this mad world
But I burn
I bloom
I fall
And freeze like ice
As I am forced to hide my beauty
Fade my truths into the back of my mind
Turn the other cheek to their wicked ways
Listen to my inner needs and wants in secret
And sometimes I even melt away
Like how seasons change
But this pain always remains the same.

The Reason

I write because I cannot
hear
live
speak
or see
life's beings any other way.

Artist

My heart and mind align
in perfect times
To remind me
I am an artist.

Expressful Creativity

Art cannot carve something new from pain
onto my fearful heart
as I search for a peace of mind

My religion is what lead me to the light
as I was trapped in the darkness
and the hope is present amongst the distress

I look for a home within
a throne to print my name upon
as I express myself through my creativity

But I am no Michelangelo, Bukowski, or Gaga.

Better Person

I apologised for things I never did
To try and bring peace to situations
I had no control over.

I don't want to be that person anymore
I feel an awakening happening in this evolution
To be a better person for me.

Sisterhood

In this unsafe world
Our worries heighten
When we leave to go home

It's all fun and games
Until the protective side kicks in
Making our sacred bond our security

We say, *hold your keys in between your fingers*
Be aware of your surroundings
Text me when you get home

The enforcing fierceness of love
Proves competition only destroys our vision
And togetherness is something powerful.

Balance

How could I fear someone so beautiful and sacred?
That my mother grew in her womb
And birthed two powerful and wonderful souls
Of men I adore.

I am not afraid of the opposite sex
I am terrified of the lifeless souls
That wander into my mind and surround my body
And take what is not being offered.

Ocean of Emotions

I felt like a fish
Swimming up on every man's shore
As I was never able to
Vow to find another lover
In a sea of endless desires
That would float another fisherman by my stream
Before I could blink again
Wash the pain away
And surrender the ocean of emotions
That kept me from processing the tragedies of my life.

Need to Fit In

I don't need to go out
Out of my immediate comfort zone
To drink everyone under the table
Have a list of endless mistakes
Regretting these actions when I wake
To be the end game of someone's satisfaction
Because I have many skeletons hidden deep within
But they no longer scare me
Only fuel the desire to live on my own terms;
I no longer feel the need to fit in to belong.

Wake Up Call

All the abuse I suffered
Found me then becoming an abuser to myself.

I thought I deserved ever beating
But I got a wake up call.

It's time for me to make up for lost time
And mend old broken roads of bridges I burnt.

Small Appetite

These days I have a small appetite
I keep myself fed
Denying the hunger of men
Who think I am blind to their narcissism.

Taking Charge

When the deluded feeling
Of thinking, he was my first love
Set in the notable realisation
Proved he had nothing more to offer
But childish games where he pulled my long hair
That he was nothing more than a boy learning to walk
And not yet a man to hold my hand
Or tame the lioness inside me
I was a fierce creature
Out of the womb and ready for life I cut my hair short
To show who was in charge.

Lasting Revenge

The lasting revenge of all
Is I am no longer yours

I am no longer one half piece of a whole
I am my own and grateful for the painful escape

For this punishment lives on in your head Forevermore
you are drenched in regret.

Eternity of Desirable Dreams

I am not a novel read in one sitting.

A conversation over dinner where you think you know
everything about me.

I am much more than a one night stand where you are
unfazed by the quick and easy pleasure.

I am not a receipt tossed aside
When you are done with the good

I am not labelled to one thing
But an eternity of desirable dreams

.

Small Doses

I give myself in small doses
But I am an open book
What you see is what you get
I will answer what you ask
But once we part ways
It will hurt less since we never intertwined
I no longer feel the need to confess
Every detail of my life.

What He Wants

There is nothing sexier
Then a man who knows what he wants
Rather than a boy who is unfazed, unfocused
And plays me like a guitar
I am no musical instrument with strings
Tied to my heart for them to play
I am worth more than this
I deserve a man who can look me in the eye
And tell me what he wants.

Kiss the Scars

His lips kiss the scars
That were caused way before his appearance

On my mind
On my body
On my soul

Everything and more that I had apologised for endlessly
in the arms of others.

Waves

I rise
and fall
for you
like
the sea.

From the Heart

When I was young
I grew up being afraid of everything
From the darkness of the night
To the jungle of reptiles hidden among us
That would soon take our lively bodies
And surrender to death

Until one day I met you
And now I fear losing you.

Not a Lesson

I can only guess what we were
Because there are two points of views
Two different perspectives on the same company
But I am certain we felt the same, to some extent
That we collided perfectly, and together as one
Becoming more than a sinful confession
We made it more than I could have ever imagined
And for that, you were a blessing
Not a lesson.

Learning the Lessons

I changed myself so much for each relationship
To a point I could no longer recognise myself
Taken to a strange place
Stripped back from all I had known
Unappreciated and torn apart
Treated like I was nothing

I had to walk away
Rebuild my life back up
And get to know me all over again
For no one will ever love me more
Or be there through it all But me.

Fisherman

We are powerful
But we bend and break
Through heartache
And that's okay
There are plenty more stories to be written
And much more fish in the sea
That leads you to your fisherman.

Needs

My body and mind are too precious
To present to someone
Without seeing consistent signs
And pleasure that match my needs.

The attention that is sought
Will never fall into one's lap
Without consistency and loyalty;
The keys to unlock my respect and time.

Breaking the Cycle

I sit with myself
And search through my life
Trying to find
Something that defines
The wrongdoings
Inflicted on me
But I then come to realise
These actions by the faithless
Are an endless cycle
That I must break.

Loud in the Silence

I will not be wasteful of my words
That can cut like a sharp knife
Or heal wounds that bleed through

I will keep my conversation meaningful
And all the things I don't have words to describe
I will show you with my actions

For the fact that I kept myself back
Biting my tongue in rage
To stay sane and present

In a moment that I felt unworthy
Only taught me to speak up
Or forever let the unsaid drill sorrow into me.

Best I Go

I leave silently
Without making much noise
As the delicate rush of ache
Tenders my heart
The restless and misery feeling
Overwhelms me into a delusion;
It's for the best I go
And never return.

No Choice

To the ones I left
I apologise for I had to love myself
The way you promised;
But failed to.

I now see
You are incapable of love me
A tender soul with a lot of potential;
You left me no choice.

Forgiveness

I had to forgive each character in my life
That left open wounds and knots within me
To cleanse my soul
And do what is right for me
To alleviate the wrongdoings by other
That I don't have control over.

Poetic License

The poetic license I hold
Finds my imagination running wild
Turning a raindrop into an ocean
Feeding my ego with passion
Thinking its love
Telling the one I adore their royalty
So never trust a poet
For we create an alternative universe
In which every curse becomes bearable.

Behind the Scenes

I work behind the scenes in silence
Never stepping out of place
Or getting in anyone's way

And when I take a pen to paper
I let the rage flow out
And roar like a lioness

For the beast within me is tamed
And let to roam free through my words.

Success in Tragedy

The success found in tragedy
Will never find closure
Only the disinterest in a situation
That leaves us longing for more
But in time knowing we deserve greater things
than feeling less than we are.

Growth

I knew I would never get an apology
And I never expected them to say they are sorry
But the fuel I could have used to enlighten more pain
I found serenity in forgiveness and love
As the growth set me free
I found the courage to let them go.

Globe

And like a globe
I found myself in a new world
Protecting my heart this time
While living my life for me;
Carefree and reckless.

Happy Accidents

We save each other by accident
As the earth turns and blooms
With a strangers smile
A kind gesture
A helping hand of a loved one
A baby's laugh
A friendly face in a time of need
A joke to bring us back to where we are
In a split moment of shared attention
Tangling souls to realise we are not alone
Living, breathing, being.

Timelessly

Life will shatter timelessly
But it is you who rebuilds the city around you.

The nightmares will wake you up in cold sweat
But you are in control.

And there is no doubt it will happen again
Because it will.

Be ready to surrender
And bloom beautifully.

Worthy of Love

I let go of the narcissistic traitors
The ones who dragged me down
The ones who kept me at my worst
The ones who abandoned me
And only remembered my name in time of need.

I let go of the past that held me back
In order to find my best self
Because I am worthy of love.

Begin Again

Art is cheaper than therapy
I paint the pain upon an empty canvas
Stroking the brush over the hurt
Filling in the blanks
Piecing together the reckless feeling
Realising what I have lost
But it will not break me
Or shatter my heart
As it is a fresh start
When I finish
another piece And
begin all over again.

Mourning

Selfish

I come from a place
Where separation is embedded in my blood
Of people who don't talk
Living through silence
That starves my being
Suffocating my expectations
That get crushed
Where my scream go unnoticed
And I was never enough to satisfy
Their selfish needs.

All I've Ever Known

I was the toy tossed around when I was a child
Thrown back and forth from places
So forgive me
I never learned the true ways of life
To stay and fight for something
Only the dark side
Where I learned their wicked ways
Learning to escape the mess
Crawling deep into my mind
Closing off the shutters
Letting no one in
Shutting off
And forgive me when I give up
It's all I've ever known.

Lonely Hour

I yearn to be healed
At the feet of those who hurt me.

I let anyone in to fill the void
And take my mind off things.

But the pain is visible in my eyes
Yet I hope their intentions are good;

In my lonely hour.

Deepest Fear

I exposed myself to my deepest fear When
I realised I am alone in a world full of hate
But surrounded by dark hearts.

I stopped communicating and begging for a relationship
With someone who refuses to see past their problems
That they project on me.

But each line I draw
Finds them pushing and pulling me away
making me feel I am the problem.

These signs don't align right away
Their addictive personalities drain my every being
sucking the light out of my soul.

I am left fragile, abandoned and all alone
But I work hard to recover from this loss
To be the best version of myself.

With self-care and preservation
I know it's possible to heal
But it never works unless one decides to.

The First Man

Will you ever forgive him for breaking your heart?
The first man to swallow and crush you all at once.

The one who was supposed to show you what you
deserve
And love you like no other.

Only to deny your existence
Making you feel like every problem he caused was your
fault.

As the memories stained your innocence
I just hope you know you're worth so much more.

Than a false relationship where you try and try again Until
your heartaches and bones break.

Conditional Love

You don't understand that when I talk and you cut me off
When you rant on about something that is irrelevant
And use my past against me
Of my failed relationships
And lessons I learned the hard way
Hardships that broke me in two
But repaired me into the version of the person I am today
From living in the past, being stuck
To living presently in the here and the now
I close off from the world around me
I don't need advice or for you to fix my problems
I just need a hand to hold
A positive light that life gets better
Instead of tearing every inch of my being apart
But the hatred in your eyes defines your angst against me
You love me with conditions
Not unconditionally.

Selfish Desires

An addict as a parent is not a parent
For they do not put others before their selfish desires
To kill their veins and slather their livers
And choose everything above their children
That they once made with love.

Sobriety is foreign
And being clean is a forgotten feeling
They never gave their children a chance
They never raised these souls
To be something more than the neglect.

This Feeling

The people around me
When I was growing up
Believed in things
I could not understand
Or be convinced of.

One thing was for sure
Love was to be fought for
During trying times
And conquered in desperate times
No matter the circumstances.

I used to indulge in the fascination
To cherish every soul I would ever know
But then someone crushed my faith
And I gave up on this feeling
That once intrigued me.

Begging

I'm tired of pleading for a relationship
with a higher authority
To someone that should have been
My first love and everything in life
But they are the aching cracks in my bones
The anxious shakes
The dooming feeling of despair
The loneliness I feel in his empty presence
I long for more with the expectation that things will change
But my broken heart knows what we once had
Is now lost and beyond repair
I used to turn to him like a best friend
And I never saw the world any different
Until my life changed at a young age
Spiralling out of control in their hands
Each phone call hung up, cut off and lead to voicemail
Each passing met with silence
And wondering endless what ifs
Each conversation turned to hatred, blame and disgust
Filling me with shame
And passed down generational problems
To a point, I feel my existence was a mistake
But then I realise I never asked to be here
I have learned the hard way
That no one should have to beg for a relationship.

Open Heart

I grew up with an open heart in silence
Listening to those before me
Never speaking out of turn
Only when spoken to
For my mouth never knew another way.

I learned patience from a young age
And how good things take time
But I was born tender into a rough world
With a vulnerable soul that lives life to its fullest
And I never had the privilege to choose me

Somebody

My neglected soul
Has never felt love
Or the nurturing feeling
I desperately feel I deserve

But as I brush through the cobwebs
I find beauty in the trauma
A life worth living
A soul shattered but mending;

Somebody.

Lust for Love

He wanted my body
Never feeding my soul
And nothing more
Because he had a passion
To be irrational
Confusing lust for love.

Disease of Heartache

I am drenched in the disease of heartache
of being a hopeless romantic
and my own worst enemy
at the best of times
so please don't make me fall in love
only to slowly watch you disappear.

Wandering Eyes

I noticed his eyes wandered
To everyone around me.

He was a drifter
Floating from girl to boy.

Searching for someone different and more
And once I left.

He lost his home and final destination of happiness
Once he discovered our hearts connected like no other.

Young Love

These scars are self-inflicted wounds
Of a young love weapon
And a souvenir
That rips my heart open
When I think of him.

Feeling Your Absence

My heart throbs
at the sounds of your name

My heart breaks
from the memories

And I feel the heavy pain
a little more than before

As I sit at the edge of my bed
feeling your absence.

Wrong Person

Every time he told me he loved me
I always felt it sounded wrong

It came from the wrong person.

Ungrateful and Wrong

I lost myself many times in relationships
To people who didn't respect me
Where I had to compromise and sacrifice
My entire life to make it work
To please their wants and needs
At the cost of my sanity and livelihood
In order to fit perfectly in the hands of
The ungrateful and wrong person.

The Intruder

The intruder was someone I knew
Someone who knew my every move
Watching and catching me off guard
He had the key
So I wasn't afraid, at first
When he gained my trust
Only to lose it in a matter of seconds

Like when a house is on fire
You know to run
You don't stop to solve the problem
When it's escalating before your eyes
But I froze and felt paralyzed
In a moment of sacrifice
To lose my judgment, will and life

And all power of my body and mind
He took my lifeline
As I fell deep into a dark hole
Struggling to escape, but I was trapped
In the delusion of his illusion
When he took my story away
But I fought to get my life back.

Forbidden Fruit

I've sadness
in places
he touched.

Consent

Was my consent ever enough?
I said no.

I wonder will my body ever heal
From the trauma of you.

Bag of Bones

I grew used to the abuse
Almost immune to your sharp words
And fingers like thorns slicing my insides
It was predictable on what to expect
As I laid there in the silence shocked and paralyzed
While you carved me as your next victim
Someone who lost their voice
Didn't have the encouragement to speak up
Or bravery to fight against someone as cruel as you
I was just a bag of bones to you.

Tragedy Laid Upon Us

Day by day I become more immune
And unafraid of these monsters
Scattering themselves through these streets
Because of the sad matter of fact
And appalling truth of it all
Is that it could be any of us
Facing a lifelong sentence
Of our innocence being taken
With no justice to repair
The broken state of mind
And bruises heal and scars fade
But the memories will remain
As a reminder of the tragedy laid upon us.

Appalling

A woman birthed them into life
But they see us as a clowder of cats
In a society that tells them
It's okay to whistle and catcall us.

When it's not okay
And it never will be okay
To open their foul mouth
And speak of such shame
In an appalling manner.

First Home

She tore her body apart for his child
Making her vulnerable and responsible for this life
Protecting her womb with her every being
And he is ungrateful for her existence
His essence was formed within a woman
Created too by his own kind
But he still turns around calling her weak
Forgetting where his first home was.

Undeniably Irreplaceable

Men have hurt me
And pushed me beyond the breaking point
To a place where the feeling is undeniably irreplaceable
But it reflects their personal indifference

They want to hurt
They want to torture
They want to pain
They want it all

And forget that sadly this isn't what I want.

Issues

Men reflected my innermost issues
The insecurities I dare to forget most

My fears
My past
My daddy issues

They wanted me dressed to the nines
Portray me as a mannequin

Instead, I longed for love, trust and something more
Something they could never offer.

Bittersweet Disaster

I tried to swallow your name
And keep it down
But it was brought up
Like a sickness
When I kept coughing
Until the pain ended

It almost felt like I was hiding the truth
Like a child with a secret
From their parent
But it unfolded
I came clean
The visible honesty painted upon my face

You were my worst nightmare
My best kept secret
Until it came to light again
The love, heartache, and dearest tragedy
All filled me up until I confessed
The bittersweet disaster.

Retelling the Tales

In moments with other bodies
I share too much
With invisible ink splattered across my memory
Ticking each moment off
As I retell the tales of my life
To another lifeless soul
That won't be here tomorrow.

Ruined by Mankind

I felt like a girl ruined by mankind
False-hearted ones who imprinted
The intrusive actions on my body
That will forever stain my memory
But I rise each morning like the sun
Still fearing to explore the world
Only to be potentially hurt by another one.

Collateral Damage

No man destroyed me
No hurt caused by the reflection
of their character tamed me
Their words, fear, emotional intertwining negligence
never worked for me
In the end only to figure out
The destroyed man
Lost his way and strength
Thinking portraying the pain on me
would help I was just collateral damage.

Wicked Man

He was beyond repair
The horrible sinking feeling I felt in his presence
Should have been enough for me to leave

But I felt I had to stay
In the devilish arms of a wicked man
Who treated me like I was nothing.

Wicked Ways

I sugar coated the truth
And lied to me
Making him out to be a better man
As I edited his wicked ways
Censored his harsh words
Rearranged our history so it wouldn't seem so cold
Until it, all weighed me down
The burden got too much to carry
I had to finally make things right
And set me free
And realise I deserved better than he ever gave me.

Mother

I told him off
And put him in his place
Not thinking about the estrangement
Or the role I would fore take
For his behaviour caught a nerve
But he listened and learned
Before he looked at me as his mother.

The Bleak Aftermath

The way he left
Told me everything
I needed to know
About the person, I slept beside
In the dead of the night
Scared out of my mind.

Nostalgia

I made friends with a bottle or two
Each time I thought of him
Sipping on nostalgia
Staying up all night watching the previous day wither away
Like the roses, he got me for my birthday
I continue to reminisce on what could have been
As another day blooms in front of me
But the memories are nothing more than bittersweet
Yet I get so high on the melancholic feeling
Drenched in regret come morning light
As the truth fades into view
Surrounded by empty bottles
And not him.

Empty Bed

I couldn't sleep alone for the longest time
So I drifted into bed with lovers
Through different times
When my mind would wonder
Pausing time to rethink the trauma
Freezing me into thinking it was happening all over again
But they left like they always do
And I'm left here curled up in this loneliness
Facing another sleepless night
In this empty bed.

Uncertainty

I waited and wondered
While you left to discover
What you wanted
And I knew it was never me

But I knew all
along All I
ever wanted
Was your certainty.

Endless Sheets

He only wondered about me
When he had roamed through endless sheets
Searching for someone better
than me
Something more than we had
And came up empty.

Remembering to Forget

I choose men that are nothing like you,
In comparison to you
Who choose women that are everything like me.

The difference is;
You want to remember,
And I want to forget.

Me Without You

I grew deaf to you to your demands
And selfish needs that caused me such misery.

I hear you and I still care for you
But need distance to repair me without you.

Big Bad Wolf

My parents censored the bedtime stories
they read to me as a child

Once I grew up and re-read the same fairy tales
and lived life through endless amounts
of love and heartbreak

That is when I understood why
they kept me from the big bad wolf.

Unfinished Business

The only thing I can rely on is a goodbye
But I'll always have unfinished business
With the collateral damaging souls
I've come across.

Resilience and Strength

He tells me there's a line
And I cross it every time
But all I hear is,
I don't believe you
It's your fault
You asked for it
And it breaks me to see myself become a victim
In his eyes
Of a crime, I did not commit or participate in.

I wasn't allowed to grief
Or cry a tsunami for the pain inflicted on me
As my knees hit the floor
The flooding emotions had to be bottled up
Stored away and never to be thought about again
And he calls me weak
Tells me what to do
But it's never good advice
On how to live after all I've been through.

But it was my resilience and strength
That found me becoming a survivor despite it all.

Survivors

The fear of judgment and isolation
Is what kept me from coming forward, again

I never asked to be harassed or assaulted
In any manner
But this is the world that we live in

A cruel place where victims of these actions hide the
shameful display
Of another's pathetic ways

To almost protect ourselves
From more traumatic experiences
While troubling our dignity and well being

But we are survivors
Our strength unites us
As the devastation tears us apart

And there is love
Even if it's inside us.

A Compliment Battle

Before
I felt I had to
Spread my legs
Open my heart
And shut my mouth
Whenever a man complimented me.

Flesh

My flesh wants you
But my mind is triggered by flashbacks
Of the memories and pain, he caused
For each touch is a reminder
Back to a time I wish to forget
I don't know if you can ever erase a theft
As the scars and bruises fade visibly
Forever remaining broken inside
Afraid to let anyone in
But just know I want you
I just don't know how to have you.

Burden

I talk, but I am silenced
And the day I kept my pain inside
Was the day I became a survivor, not a victim.

And I agree, but not wholeheartedly
As the hidden hurt finds the truth buried beneath
The dirt and gravel in an unmarked grave.

And voicing my emotions heal my inner self
I never expect anyone to relive the trauma
Or carry the burden.

Play the Victim

I didn't play the victim
To the way they wanted me to
For my performance was real
And not staged for their convenience.

They doubted me in reaction to
My forthcoming confession
Of an unforgettable event
I witnessed first-hand.

They didn't believe me
Because I didn't show emotion
As I felt dead inside
With only cold nights insight.

I was blind to the world around me
Yet I felt the freezing touches
That paralyzed my body
As my mind escaped to save my soul.

They weren't empathic
Knowing I suffered from Stockholm syndrome
Laying in the hands of my abusers
Frozen and dead to the world as I feared the worst.

And how dare I survive
Not knowing their intentions
Eventually coming out the other side
Given time to flourish to feel free and alive.

Thrilling and Terrifying

I take caution and care
To the world around me
While I stay vigilant and aware
Paying attention to the little details
While trying to live
But the intriguing feeling
Thrills and terrifies me
That I cannot feel alive and happy
All at the same time.

Mysterious Tragedy

A goodbye is easy
With a quick spill of the tongue
But it's the aftermath
That evolves the truth and pain
Embedded inside the mind
Consuming the insides
Tangling reality and the past as one
With a mysterious tragedy in plain sight.

Awe and Unknown

I don't write about intimate moments
That revolved around my passion, lust and more
Because they are trapped in private places Hidden away in
my memory.

I don't talk about two bodies intertwined as one
For my survival and silence holds me together like a
tightrope
That my skin, my body, my bones will forever hold back
Built in this person I am today.

I don't discuss the meat flesh sinners who took advantage
For the very same monsters will try to banish my bravery
And come back to show me how afraid I can be Because it
is the only thing that terrifies me.

I religiously confide in my writing
But this is something even paper has yet to find out
For I will never reveal what the evil ones did
What their cravings did once they seen the fear in my
eyes.

I live my life silently
Going about my days as best as I can
Feeling the numbness, passion, shame, and hope
I remain in the darkness filled with the awe and unknown.

Soft Landing

In a soft landing
Of my tears falling on my pillow
I close my eyes when I cry
Hiding from the world around me
protecting myself
So I can't see the hurt
And how bad the pain hurts.

Secrets and Shame

I remain embedded in fear and hope
Raged between this war inside me
And the will to live with secrets and shame
Hidden deep inside of thing I should say
But never seem to do
I eat myself alive
Rather than spitting the truth.

Irish Goodbye

Closure remains embedded
As something I feel I need
To move on.

To forgive and forget
I remain the same
But armoured with growth.

When visitors come and go
Leaving with an Irish goodbye.

Magic

The disappearing act
Which men I know are best at
Is proof that magic is real.

Trace of You

Hide tides crashed against my heart
And brought you into my life

The currents swept you out
Leaving me stranded

I tossed and turned through each night
Losing grip on what was in plain sight

You would go, leave and let me heal
And then return, coming back to make me feel it all, again

The water filled my heart with more ache
Until you disappeared for good

And washed away any trace of you.

The Wrong Hands

I was in the hands of men
Who wasn't man enough
To treat me in such a way
Where I felt good enough
Or worthy of love. . .

The wrong hands make you question yourself.

Bad Taste

The bad taste stains my mouth
After telling him 'I love you'.

It is a lie
for the distasteful manner of my judgment is wrong.

For I never loved him
And I never will.

Someone Like Me

I was attracted to unavailable men
Taken by the beauty in the suffering
Of someone like me.

Dissatisfied Standards

I rebelled against my heart
Each time I found comfort
In a lover's dissatisfied standards.

But I have learned the hard way
I will never find myself letting
people take the best parts of me.

Never Leave

The more they tell me
They want me to stay
The more I am in disbelief
For if they wanted to stay
They would never leave.

The Slow Death

One day at a time
I watch you fade away
Deep into my memory
Cutting through my heartstrings
Removing every inch of your soul
That once tangled itself in mine

I feel the slow torture of letting you go
Moment by moment
And it's difficult losing someone I've loved
As I took a wrong turn
Falling into the arms of a regretful lover

The extraordinary ending
Found me looking back, in hindsight
Remembering the good, the bad
And the indifferent
As life reveals itself before me
In a delicate, yet fascinating way

You were my wildest journey
A failed love attempt
And once our bond broke
Something in me died.

Outgrowing Tragedy

The nerves hit as the silence broke down
In its golden moment
As I laughed nervously in the anticipation
Of running away from this mess
Striking a match,
Burning up the place,
And watch it turn to ash
I promised the ungrateful ones the world
With no questions asked to keep them on side
I gave my all until my last breath
But it was never enough
As they threw me on board the shipwreck
The feeling of disaster made me survive
I have outgrown the tragedy
And the lifeless faces of the traitors
Will never fill the empty seats
At the dinner table of my past
And the justice system inside my head
Fade their blurry faces and crimes away
I never want to think of them again.

Scared to Love

I'm scared to love again
And fall back into the same old patters
That once led me into the wrong arms.

Redemption

Like a lost child
I only saw the good in things
Believing in the greater good
During the calm before the storm.

But once the infectious disease
Got a hold of me
Sweeping me off my feet
Breaking, crackling and demolishing me.

I discovered the endless cycle
That the poisonous souls that reached my heart
Underneath layers of brokenness
Searched for redemption, too.

Catastrophic Weight

The catastrophic weight in my chest
Numbs me from a reality I desperately want to face
It feels like my mind and body are shut off
Closed off from the world to protect my fragile soul
For the sadness remains embedded
And the impatience destroys every being in me
That stops me from healing.

Where I Leave You

In the death of our past
In the beautifully chaotic present
In the wait of our future;

With the love
The loss
And everything in-between;

This is where I leave you.

Healing

All At Once

It's a beautiful thing
Breaking and healing
All at once.

Someone Like This

You found me when I was in the dark
All alone with this sadness.

You loved me from the very start
Through all the madness.

I thought something like this
Would never happen to someone like me.

New Beginnings

There are exciting adventures ahead
With fresh conversations
And much more to expect

The eye may deceive what the heart wants
But the sudden rush of happiness
Of knowing I am

Ready to commit
Hungry for love
And thirsty for lust

That I crave something worthwhile
A little sweet and divine
Wholeheartedly knowing it's mine

As the sugar coated lies are forgotten
As this new found bliss finds me blushing
Fulfilling my desires;

It's true and this moment belongs to me.

The First Time

I need a little loving
Something to shake my heart
Break the silence
Hold me close
Cut through the shyness
Pierce the loneliness
Make my soul feel alive
Something I have never had before.

And for the first time
I know what I want.

Liberating Love

We formed a connection
Through our hearts and intellect
That engages us deeper than desire and lust
I treasure your touch, your smile
And everything that aligns when we're together
The liberation of being with someone
Who challenges me, my every move, and my being
Rather than restricting my drive and fire within
Has found my heart falling for the spontaneous soul
That allows me to grow, flourish
And release all tension that wouldn't let me escape
Or chase after my dreams;
With you I am free.

Our Story Binds Us

You're the silver lining
And the reason why I continue.

Your voice is serenity
And the clarity I need.

You're the armour
Ruling over the darkness I conquer.

You're the light and love
For better or worse, I follow;

Our story binds us.

Treasurable Times

As a child, my parents read fairy tales to me
Before bed to escape my innocence
Into a life beyond imaginable
And it wasn't until I grew up
When I figured out
Short stories are treasured the most.

My Medicine

Writing is my medicine
To help me cope with my mental health.

It is something that consumes every part of me
That I capture my thoughts and emotions through my
words.

I pour everything out it supports me through
My mental bruising, physical shakes, and irritable
emotions.

My brain calms down when I take a moment to say;
I am here and I am safe.

Work in Progress

I am a work in progress
My life is a chaotic mess
I have been thoughtless and careless
I have lived through uncertainty
My insanity really gets to me
This beautiful trauma
And these unbelievable moments
My life will follow me to the grave
But they have shaped me
Into the person I am today.

Luminous

I am luminous
In old photographs that capture a time in my life
To a point where I thought I was in love
Only to lose my mind in dazzling eyes
That blurred the lines
I never stood a chance
Until I escaped
Like the moon and the stars come morning;
The light found me.

Self Love (Part I)

I am content in the arms of my own
In the company of mine

It's a dangerous thing to compete with
When you realise no fight will be won

Other than my love for my own. . .

Revolution

In the revolution where I stood tall
Unapologetically and fearlessly
Gathering my every being
I looked in the mirror
And stared at my reflection
As I declared 'I love myself'.

Recovering to Survive

When you start loving yourself
And living your life

People who once tried to control you
And manipulate you into the living

By their ways of life
Begin to become frustrated

That you value yourself
And know your worth

Instead of begging on your knees
For them to tell you how to act

But the defeat and release of freedom
Is a loss to them

And knowledge in the recognition and recovery
That you survived.

Therapeutic

I gained control in putting myself back together
After all the unfaithful souls wronged me
And it was therapeutic
Healing and showing myself the love they couldn't.

Dream

I once had a dream to become everything I wanted to
But as life got in the way with a series of unfortunate
events
Those said wishes dashed and divided
Into a million little pieces
Like shattered glass after a heartbreak
But I continued to shine and sparkle upon the pain
And watched it fade into the distance
Like stars meeting the morning sky
It occurred to me to lose everything is a must
On the road to self-discovery, living, and freedom.

Freedom in Fear

The freedom of fear
Is when I open old wounds
And cream the pain at the top of my lungs
Feeling every emotion rush through my blood;
I am alive.

Beautiful Disaster

Alike to a rainstorm
I know I will land
Eventually
Like a mess
A beautiful disaster.

We Are Alive

The world isn't always heavy and bad
Or sugar coated down with metaphors and similes
Like poetry written in our bones
Like tattoos journaling on our bodies
But the blood, feeling and raw emotions
Lead us to a pleasurable comfort
knowing We are alive.

Cleansing

The natural beings
Of rain falling down
Then clearing away
Washing all good and pain away
Is like when I weep
Sometimes tears of joy
But the sadness cleanses me.

Surrendering

The claustrophobic moment of our existence
As we surrender to one another
Is a beautiful thing.

Time to Heal

The cracks you left inside me
Have bloomed beautifully
Finding me in a better time
Where I find peace to heal
Knowing I escaped something
That painfully hurt me.

Complicated

Men think I am complicated
For the simple fact
I want more than a one night stand
I want a man and not just a boy
I want something more than a fling
I want to scream at the top of my lungs
'I am in love'
And all these men who have this opinion of me
Were never worth my time or energy.

Damsel

I am not a damsel in distress,
I am capable of rescuing myself.

Who I Am

I am not collateral damage
Of misfortunate events.

I am made up of every experience
That makes me stand tall;

Unapologetically and fearlessly.

Relatable

Once I learned
Love, hate and everything in between
Is familiar in all the ways it happens

It's the breaking moments that feel isolated
That this is only happening to me
With the lessening of love

And devastation
And longing
And healing

It shows me this is what I feel
Me without you.

Self Love (Part II)

Through each trauma, heartbreak, and life change
I remained evolving and growing
I never gave up on myself
For self-love is a beautiful thing
Knowing I break and heal endlessly.

Beautiful Trauma

I kissed the pain
With a paintbrush
Upon the canvas
Creating art
From the beautiful
trauma Held inside me.

Loving the World

I always believed in the good in people
No matter the amount of times I've been hurt
Or how many times I've been burnt
I learned in the process of healing
Those who turn my love into pain
Need love themselves
For the conflicting actions aren't set off by me
It all gives me the strength to proceed
To love the world around me.

Water

I have the power like water within me;
With a soft touch to cleanse you,
With enough force to drown you
And enough depth to save you,

The One Who. . .

The one who betrayed you
who hurt you
who caused you to lose the light in your eyes
who has never apologised for the pain and broke you
does not deserve mercy
or a place in your memory
to unfold when time trigger memories
but to be forgotten
while you find hope and courage to heal to breathe
To fall in love and rediscover
yourself because you will survive.

I am Here and I am Safe

They feel more at home in my body than I ever have
And those tragic nights where I fear my own life
Are those times I survive myself.

I am my own worst enemy
Knowing the beauty remains as I create more
Building upon the strength I courageously found.

After the monstrous separation of my innocence when no
consent was given
There is no justice, but there is healing.

I want to reclaim my body, my voice, my home I want to
feel I belong, rather than feeling distant Like I have
forgotten who I am.

I am here and I am safe
I whisper to myself
Regaining my own trust, identity, self-worth, and love.

I am worthy of all I rebel again with this pain.

Moments of Clarity

The hurt caused by the narcissistic traitor held me back
But my resilience and curiosity got the better of me
Saving me from a time
I thought I would never escape from
I know I can't hold on to everything
It's a hard thing to swallow
Knowing the poison and cure is everywhere around me
I have the right to choose and be picky
With whom I associate myself with
For it is my life that I live
I look for strength, love, and recognition of my presence
An eye of a bold stranger sometimes fills my heart with joy
Compared to the italic people around me.

I become intertwined in the traits of a romantic
And grow fondly intact in them
Removing the tainted stains on my mind from a
manipulator
It's a wonderful thing to forget for a little while and own it
I have outgrown some who will not let me go
Tied to me like a rope
I have no issue cutting the bad ones off like split ends
And ghosting them until they finally get the message
Seeing me burn brighter than the morning sun
I would walk down familiar places rekindling past
memories
And the flashbacks would stop me on my steps
To somewhere new, shaking steadily.

Like the tears, they caused soon dried
Finding self-love and my self-respect
In a moment of clarity.

Note to Self

your pain is valid. your voice isn't blocked out by the noise of others. but your silence will drain and tear you apart. and your strength will see you overcome your greatest tragedy. you are the main character in your life. and although sometimes you go unheard. tune in to yourself. value your intimate moments. breathe. look around. you're safe. alone in your presence. don't shine away from being the brave soul you know you are. time will heal the ripping wounds. but the lesson will forever be learned and remembered. hidden away in a box at the back of your mind. only opened once triggered. it's a coping mechanism. your intelligence will lead you to good health. but first, you must break. lose yourself and everything around you. then surrender. and let go. because your story isn't over yet.

Grounded

I sit quiet absorbing the world
Grounded in every inch of my being
Escaping with the adventurous feeling
Every chance I get
And I doubt myself the most
When happiness comes along
My inner dialog tends to create anxiety
That was once pushed aside
I've learned the importance of being alone
And finding moderation over time
In a disastrous time where my wildest dreams
Became a nightmare
And it's the truth about life and suffering
That when I begin to move on
It finds me in the coldness in the fresh air
The bittersweet taste of moments of nonchalant
The conversations that's been and gone
Triggered by a memory
Taking a step back to see my life in hindsight
Played back like I could change something
But I can't
They never appreciated my love, existence
Or anything I had to offer
Rather they preferred to ruin and wreck
My self-esteem and broken dreams
And trauma does not define
But creates the strength to carry through.

Intelligent

I am an entitled soul
Alike to the rest of the world
With a voice, a mind, a story to share.

I fought for my right to not be
defeated I am stronger than
they all thought I am one.

My intelligence is worn like a fine wine
A beautiful accessory
The light bottle, a ritual
Alike to a simple act of remembering one's
duty.

My only job is to love myself
While ignoring their ignorance
Fearing their treads, revealing truths
A shadow less echo remained unspoken.

Although my heart might be stupid at times I
remain innocent, childlike to the world around
me
During the exciting changes.

I am courageous
I am loving
I am intelligent.

Recovery Time

The weight of the absence
Of someone I adored so greatly
Found me suffering in silence

The deeply traumatic events I experienced by their side
Found me growing inward
To a point the burden made my heart weary
Persevering all good intentions, to run
And never look back

It still makes me wonder why I stayed
Through the neglect and abuse
But as time unfolds and the truth reveals itself
My heart and soul find the strength to move on
And become more resilient

And it wasn't until time had passed
That the close attention lost itself in a moment of disaster
That nothing would have saved what we once had
No apology was necessary
You crossed the line

But the drunk and disorderly one
Who demanded a response to save what we once had
Found my silence as the only reaction
As I slipped through his fingertips
And into a time of recovery and saving myself.

Art of Letting Go

I have outgrown the past
But I still hurt in the present
Burying myself before the future
In a grave like those who hurl against me

This mind maze mind of mine
Watches me swallow the poison
thinking it's a cure

But falling into a stranger
Intertwining our heartstrings
It's a beautiful thing
A wonderful experience to forget
In a magical moment

Pieces fall into place
The rival's fear and loathing
Turn the damned into beauty

The rejection, heartbreaks, and lessons
Are all a learning process
And the art of letting go
Is an act to move on.

Let Go

Sometimes I feel I'm grieving
For those, I've outgrown.

And that's when I know I'm healing
while letting go.

Learning

I'm still learning how to laugh again
To make noise
To be unafraid in a frightening world
To let my lost innocence find me
To stop, breathe, and look around
To realise I survived
And   that   I   am   alive.

Full in Circle

I have come full circle
It almost feels like a brand new life
As I am surrounded by the remains
Of the beautiful trauma
Which liberates my soul.

I found freedom baring my truths
The confidence to tell my secrets
And give a voice to the colourless past
Failures and rejections
While embracing my true self
As I lovingly accept
Who I am.

Toast

Here is a toast
To the past, present, and future

To all that has been before me
And yet to greet me

In all faith and fear
I stand alone daring to feel

The hope and despair
In each new beginning and end.

The End

Acknowledgements

To my parents, thank you for giving me life. I love you.

To my siblings, for giving me purpose and pride to carry on through destructive times. You will always be a hero in my story. I love you.

To my readers, this collection was once mine, and now yours. I hope this journey inspires you. And know, it's possible to find and see the light of day, again.

About the Author

Danielle Holian is an Irish writer and photographer, born in the West of Ireland. She studied media in college, moving on to flourish her creativity through art. She continues her passion for words through her media work, documenting her interests, spars and amusements as she captures moments she relives through her art.

Connect with Danielle via –

Facebook (missdanielleholian)
Instagram (danielleholian_)
LinkedIn (Danielle Holian)
Tumblr (missdanielleholian)
Twitter (danielleholian_)

Printed in Great Britain
by Amazon